Seven True
Dog Stories

Seven True Dog Stories

by MARGARET DAVIDSON

Pictures by SUSANNE SUBA

Hastings House · Publishers
NEW YORK 10016

Especially for Patrick

Second Printing, August 1979

Text copyright © 1977 by Margaret Davidson. Illustrations
pages 19–61 copyright © 1977 by Scholastic Magazines. Illustrations pages 67, 73 copyright © 1977 by Hastings House.
This edition is published by Hastings House by arrangement
with Scholastic Book Services, a division of Scholastic Magazines, Inc. All rights reserved. No part of this publication may
be reproduced, stored in a retrieval system, or transmitted, in
any form or by any means, electronic, mechanical, photocopy-
ing, recording or otherwise, without the prior permission of the
copyright owner or the publishers.

Library of Congress Cataloging in Publication Data
Davidson, Margaret. Seven true dog stories.
  Bibliography: p.
  Includes index.
  SUMMARY: A collection of seven true stories relating the
adventures of such dogs as Dox, the dog detective, Grip, a dog
thief, and Sascha, a seeing eye dog.
  1. Dogs — Legends and Stories — Juvenile literature.
[1. Dogs] I. Suba, Susanne, 1913–   II. Title.
SF426.5.D38   636.7   77-8918
ISBN 0-8038-6738-7

Published simultaneously in Canada by Saunders of Toronto,
Ltd., Don Mills, Ontario
Printed in the United States of America

Contents

About Dogs

A long, long time ago — in the days when people lived outdoors or in caves — there were no tame dogs. All the animals of the world were wild.

One of those wild animals was the wolf. Wolves roamed through the fields and forests — and were very shy and suspicious of humans. Yet from these wild wolves (and maybe some jackals and foxes too) have come all the different dogs that are pets today.

How did this happen? It might have begun like this. One day a man was hunting in the forest. He saw a wolf — and killed it with his spear. Then he heard a soft *mewing* sound coming from somewhere nearby. He looked around and saw some wolf cubs curled up in a nest. The man raised his spear once more. After all, each of the cubs would make a tasty meal. But something stopped him. He picked one of the cubs up and carried it home instead.

The cub grew into a full-grown wolf — a wolf that was partly tame. Very likely this wolf mated with another wolf someone else had raised as a pet. Before long a litter of pups was born. This happened again and again for many hundreds of years. And little by little many of these animals who lived with people began to look less and less like wolves. Some were bigger and some smaller. Some had thicker coats and some were born with short hair.

Some were very gentle and some were even fiercer than a wild wolf. These were the first dogs.

People began to realize that dogs could be *useful* in different ways. Some dogs barked a lot. Their loud warning barks kept thieves and wild animals away. Other dogs could run very fast. They helped hunters chase down their prey. Some dogs helped farmers herd other animals, like sheep and goats.

From those early days dogs have been trained to do more and more things — until today there are hunting dogs and herding dogs, watch dogs and war dogs, police dogs and rescue dogs, circus dogs, sled dogs, guard dogs and dogs to guide the blind.

Most dogs can't see too well. They see things up close but anything far away is often just a blur to them. Many scientists think that dogs are also color-blind. They can't see the many bright colors that people can. Their world is all black and white and shades of gray in between.

A dog's sense of hearing is much keener. Dogs can hear things that are happening far away. They can hear very, very small sounds too. Dogs are also able to hear very high and very low sounds — sounds people can't pick up.

But a dog's best sense by far is his sense of smell. Some scientists say that many dogs can smell a hundred times better than people. Others say they can smell many *thousands* of times better!

A dog can read all sorts of messages with his nose. He can tell if another dog or some other animal has come his way. He can tell if that animal is a friend or a stranger. He can tell if they came by recently or a long time ago. Dogs can smell things that are happening a long way away too. Some dogs can even smell what's happening two miles away — if the wind is blowing in the right direction.

Dogs are often used to help find missing people — like lost children and escaped criminals. First you give a dog something that belongs to the missing person — a shirt or a shoe or perhaps a handkerchief. The dog gives it a good sniff. Then he is taken to the spot where the person was last seen. And off he goes — his nose close to the ground. Some dogs have sniffed a missing person's trail for many miles.

For centuries dogs have been used in time of war. Dogs have smelled enemy soldiers creeping closer and closer — and so helped stop surprise attacks. During World War I many dogs were trained to find wounded soldiers left behind on a battlefield. Often the soldiers would be too weak to call out. But the dogs could sniff out where they were — even on the darkest night. This was dangerous work. More than 7,000 dogs were killed in World War I.

During World War II many dogs were trained to help find people trapped in bombed buildings. Very often they could find people who were buried so deep in the rubble they couldn't be heard — or ones who couldn't cry out at all.

Like their wolf ancestors — dogs have a very strong sense of territory. A wolf's natural territory is the den where it lives and the land around the den where it hunts for food. A dog's natural territory is his house and yard. That's why even a friendly dog will bark and maybe even bite when a stranger comes into its yard. Dogs who are defending their territory are often very brave. Dogs who invade another territory usually feel timid. One day a man saw a toy poodle chasing a St. Bernard out of its yard!

Dogs — like wolves — have a very strong sense of loyalty. Wolves live in small groups called *packs*. Each wolf in a pack cares very much about every other wolf in his pack. And every pack has a leader. All the wolves are especially loyal to him.

Many people feel that a dog treats the people he lives with as though they were his pack. That's why most dogs are so loyal to their human families. And many a dog is especially devoted to one person. That human being is the dog's special pack-leader.

Dogs will work day and night to please the people they love — and the only reward they need are a few words of praise or a pat on the head.

Of course some dogs may be a little *too* eager to please. One woman trained her dog to go to the street in front of her house. She trained him to pick up a newspaper and bring it back to the door. *"Good boy! Good boy!"* she said the first time he did this by himself. Those few words of praise went right to the dog's head. When the woman opened her front door the next morning she found *twenty-three* newspapers lying on her porch!

There are many stories of dogs doing brave things. Dogs have saved people from drowning. They have saved people from dying in fires too. Fire often breaks out in a house late at night — when people are fast asleep. Many dogs have barked and barked until they waked their families up. And often a dog will not leave a burning building until it is sure that everyone else is safely out.

Some dogs seem to be able to sense danger — before it happens. Then there are the dogs who become separated from the people they love — and somehow manage to find their way back to them again, even over hundreds of miles of strange country.

How do dogs do such strange and amazing things? Nobody knows for sure. It is one of the many questions about dogs that people can't answer yet.

Dogs show their feelings in all sorts of ways. They bark in warning or yelp with excitement. They growl in anger and howl with pain. They whine with fear or frustration. But most of the time a dog shows how it's feeling in a silent way. It talks with its body.

A dog who wants to be friends always holds his tail high and wags it hard. Sometimes he half-opens his mouth and pulls his lips back. He almost looks as if he's grinning. And often he will bound forward — and then run a few feet away. *"Play with me,"* he is saying now.

When a dog has been punished he acts very differently. He will not look at you for long — his eyes go everywhere else instead. His ears are flattened against the side of his head. His tail is tucked tight between his legs. Often he will lower his body to the ground and crawl toward you on his belly. Sometimes he raises one forepaw in the air. This doesn't mean he wants to shake hands! It's just another way a dog has of saying *"I'm sorry."*

A dog shows he's angry in many different ways. Very often he stares — or glares. His mouth is usually open — showing his sharp teeth. His ears are held up or bent forward. All four legs are stiff — so stiff he almost seems to be walking on tiptoe. And sometimes he even seems to grow bigger right before your eyes. This is because the hair on his back is rising straight up in the air!

A happy dog often rolls back and forth on the ground. Sometimes he waves his paws in the air. Or gives himself a good scratch. His eyes are usually half-closed and his face wears a dreamy, half-asleep look. This is a *very* happy dog.

So there are many kinds of dogs. There are pure-breds and mutts. Trained dogs and pets. Dogs that love to run and play. And dogs who seem happiest when they are curled up napping. But almost all dogs have one thing in common. They dearly love the people they live with. No wonder so many people say that a dog is "man's best friend"!

Dox,
the greatest dog detective in the world

The policeman just happened to be passing a pet store one day. He looked in and saw a roly-poly German shepherd pup in the window. And the pup looked back at him. The man wasn't even thinking of buying a dog. But a few minutes later he came out of the shop with the dog in his arms. "It was love at first

sight," Giovanni Maimone told his friends. And he named his new pet Dox.

Maimone worked as a policeman in the city of Turin, Italy. He decided to train Dox to help him in his work. Dox was a very smart dog. And he, like most dogs, had a good sense of smell. Maimone wanted to train Dox to find hidden things — jewels or money or people.

Maimone worked with Dox as much as he could. First he took a handkerchief and a cigarette case. They both belonged to someone Dox didn't know. And they carried the person's own special smell. Maimone hid the cigarette case behind the cushion of a big overstuffed chair. He let Dox sniff the handkerchief. "Find it, boy!" he said.

Of course Dox didn't understand — not at first. So Maimone led the dog to the overstuffed chair. He lifted the cushion — and there was the cigarette case. Dox sniffed at it. "Good boy!" Maimone said — as if Dox had found it by himself.

Very soon Dox understood exactly what was going on. Every time his master asked him to sniff something and then said, "Find it!" Dox knew he must find something that smelled the same.

Of course it was still just a game they were playing. Then one day a jewelry store was robbed. The thief escaped with many fine jewels. He'd left nothing behind — except a dirty old glove. Mai-

mone decided to take Dox along. It was time to test the dog on a real case.

When they got to the jewelry store, several other policemen were already there. One looked up and said with a grin, "Oh, I see you've brought Dox. Do you think he can lend us a paw?"

Everyone laughed. Everyone except Maimone. Quietly he asked for the glove. He let Dox sniff it. Then he said, "Find him, Dox!"

First Dox sniffed across the floor of the jewelry store. Out the door he ran, followed by Maimone and several other policemen. Dox moved slowly but steadily for several blocks. Then he came to a big highway. He started down it one way. He stopped. The busy highway was filled with so many smells — gasoline fumes and grass and rubber tires and trees. How could he possibly smell the special glove smell?

But he did. Dox sniffed by the side of the road for a minute or two. Then he set off in the other direction. He never lost the trail again. At last he turned off the highway into a narrow side street. Dox led the men to one of the houses on the street and sat down on the porch.

Maimone knocked on the door. His knock was answered by a woman with a baby in her arms. "What do you want?" she snapped.

The policemen explained. "There's no one here," she answered. "Except for *her*. . . ." She jiggled the baby in her arms. "My husband's in jail."

But Maimone was still suspicious. After all, Dox had led them right to this house. He and the other policemen kept checking. They soon found out that the woman was lying. Her husband *had* been in jail. But now he was out. A few days later the police caught him in a nearby town. He soon admitted that he had robbed the jewelry store. Then he had gone home for a few minutes to say good-bye to his wife and child.

Dox had solved his first case!

So the career of Dox, the dog detective, began. Before long the police in other towns heard about Dox. Often they asked for his help. He worked with the police all over Italy.

Other people knew the big dog too. Some of Dox's best friends were restaurant owners. On his birthday he could eat all he wanted in any one of their restaurants — free.

Maimone would lead him from one place to another. At each door Dox would stop and sniff. He'd move on until he found one that seemed to have nicer smells than all the rest. Then he would

go in for his favorite birthday dinner of spaghetti and pork.

On Dox's thirteenth birthday Maimone led him from restaurant to restaurant as usual. Dox seemed to be having an especially hard time deciding this year. "Choose, will you?" Maimone finally begged. "*I'm* getting hungry."

Just then they came to a small restaurant. Dox took a deep sniff. He became very still. Only his nose continued to twitch. He quickly pushed open the door and went inside.

But Dox wasn't interested in food. Not now. He headed straight for a man

who was sitting at a small corner table. The man kept on shoveling food into his mouth. He tried very hard to pretend he didn't see Dox. It was no use. Maimone recognized the man right away. He was a criminal who had escaped from the police. He was caught now — because Dox had remembered his human smell for more than *six* years.

Year after year Dox did his job. In fifteen years he helped catch more than 400 criminals!

"He has probably cracked more cases than any detective on the force," one police officer said. "We consider him one of our best men."

Grip,
the dog who was a thief

Grip was a friendly dog. And a friendly dog was just what Tom Gerrard wanted — for Tom Gerrard was a thief. He lived in the city of London, England, more than 300 years ago. Sometimes Tom Gerrard robbed big homes and stores. But most of all he liked to steal from people. That's what he trained Grip to do — to pick people's pockets.

First the man and the dog hid in an alley near a busy London street. And they waited. They waited until a man came by — a well-dressed man who might be carrying a lot of money.

Tom pointed at the man and softly snapped his fingers. Grip trotted out of the alley and began a happy dog's dance in front of the man.

He frisked, he wriggled, he wagged his tail. Sometimes the man just pushed past. But most people stopped to pet the friendly dog.

This was just what Grip had been waiting for. He would continue to prance and wriggle. But he was also using his nose to sniff out the smell of leather — the smell of a purse full of money.

It never took Grip long to find what he was looking for. Then his big mouth would open and close over the pocket with the purse in it. And with one powerful tug he'd tear the pocket *and* the purse away from the man's clothes!

Then Grip would dash away — leaving the man standing openmouthed. "Hey, you! Stop!" the man usually shouted. And the chase would begin.

Some of the men could run very fast. But Grip was never caught. He knew just where to go. He knew all the twisting streets and narrow alleys of London. He'd race up one and down another. Sometimes he would hide in a dark doorway until the man ran by. Then Grip would come out — and run the other way!

Grip always kept running until he was sure he was safe. Finally, with the purse still held firmly in his teeth, he would go back to the first alley where his master was waiting for him.

"Good dog, Grip!" Tom Gerrard always said as the dog dropped the purse into his hand. These few words of praise were all the reward Grip worked for.

What a team they made — the thief and the dog. Probably Tom Gerrard could have gone on stealing for many more years — if he'd been content just to pick pockets.

But Tom was a greedy man. One raw

and windy winter night he stopped a stagecoach on a road outside town. The door of the coach burst open. Three men with guns jumped out. Tom didn't stand a chance. He was captured and thrown into jail.

Poor Grip. For the next few weeks he wandered about the streets of London. The only food he ate was bits of garbage. And he slept in doorways or dirty alleys.

Then one day Grip saw a man walking down the street. He trotted up to him — and the man patted his head.

That was all the lonely dog needed. He followed the man home.

But who was this man Grip had chosen to be his next master? Was he another thief, like Tom Gerrard? Not at all. The man he picked to be his new master turned out to be the minister of a church instead!

Wolf,
the dog who saved other dogs

Wolf was not a friendly dog. He loved his master and mistress very much. But he didn't like other people. Wolf didn't seem to like other dogs either. He hardly ever played with the other collies that lived with him at Sunnybank Farm.

Wolf didn't like other dogs much, but he seemed to feel he had to take care of them. A big sign at the beginning of the farm's long, curving driveway read: "GO SLOW! DOGS RUNNING FREE!" Still, cars and trucks often would come roaring up the driveway.

Once a litter of pups chose the middle of the drive as their playground. So for hours at a time poor Wolf lay on the grass nearby. He watched the puppies race and tumble up and down the driveway. Every time he heard a car turn in from the road he got up and circled round and round the pups until they were in a tight bunch. Then he herded them off the drive.

But Wolf couldn't watch the puppies all the time. One day they were playing in the driveway as usual. A delivery truck turned into the farm. It swept around the first curve and came racing toward the pups.

Just then Wolf came out of a clump of trees across the lawn. He saw the danger the puppies were in. But the truck was coming so fast! And he was too far away to get them out of the way in time!

Wolf began to bark. He dashed a little

way toward the dogs. Still barking, he swung around and raced toward the trees again.

"Come on everyone! Chase me!" his loud bark seemed to be saying. And one after another the puppies did run after Wolf — off the driveway and away from the truck.

So the years passed peacefully at Sunnybank Farm. Wolf continued to watch over dogs who couldn't take care of themselves. The rest of the time he went his own way.

Wolf especially liked to take long walks. One warm spring afternoon he took a walk that led him to a railroad track.

Wolf knew about roads and cars. He also knew about railroad tracks and trains. He always stopped before crossing any railroad track. He would look in both directions and listen hard. Then he crossed quickly to the other side.

He did this now. He looked left and then right. He cocked his head. There was no train to be seen. But Wolf sat down to wait anyway. He must have heard the sound of a whistle in the distance.

A little brown dog walked past Wolf. The dog didn't look. He didn't listen either. He just walked onto the tracks and sat down to scratch a few fleas.

Wolf sprang up. He barked in warning. The dog just went on scratching. Then the sound of the train's whistle came again — much louder this time. And the train swept into sight!

Finally the little brown dog looked up. But *still* he didn't move. Now Wolf jumped and threw himself against the little dog. The dog flew through the air and landed in a nearby ditch.

Wolf tried to leap into the ditch too. He almost made it. But not quite. A piece of metal on the engine hit the side of his head. Wolf lay by the tracks. The dog who didn't even like other dogs very much would never move again. He had given his life to save a stranger.

Wolf's owner was a famous writer named Alfred Payson Terhune. Mr. Terhune wrote many more stories about Wolf and the other collies who lived at Sunnybank Farm. You can find these stories in your library.

Barry,
the dog who saved people

Today fine roads lead over the high mountains of Switzerland. Snow plows keep the roads open even in the worst weather. But it wasn't always this way.

Before the roads were built it was often very hard to cross over the mountains in winter. The only way was through some of the passes — pathways between the high peaks. One of these passes was called the Great St. Bernard Pass. At the highest point of the pass stood a big stone building. This was the monastery of Great St. Bernard. Monks had lived here for hundreds of years.

They helped people travel safely in the mountains.

Sometimes the monks led travelers along the narrow path through the pass. And sometimes, when wild storms raged, they searched for those who might be lost.

This could be very dangerous work. But the monks had help. A group of big, shaggy dogs called St. Bernards also lived at the monastery. This is the story of one of those dogs. Barry was his name.

Barry was born in the spring of 1800. At first he romped and rolled with his brothers and sisters. He tagged after the bigger dogs. And he ate and slept whenever he felt like it.

But soon the short mountain summer was over. The first snow fell. It was time for Barry and the other young St. Bernards to go to school. They had some very important lessons to learn.

First Barry had to learn to obey. He learned to come when the monks called him, to sit and lie down when the monks told him to. He learned how to walk in the deep snow. He learned how to turn his big paws outward — and spread the pads of his paws to keep from sinking in the snow. At first he still sank in up to his belly. But after a while he could walk on the snowy crust without breaking through.

Now it was time for harder lessons. Barry learned to lead people through the pass even when the narrow path was buried under many feet of snow. And he learned one of the hardest lessons of all — to find people who might be lost in a storm.

If the person could walk, Barry led him back to the monastery. But sometimes a person would be hurt — or weakened by the cold. Then Barry raced back to the monastery to lead the monks back to the spot.

He also learned to search for people who were lost *under* the snow. Sometimes an avalanche — a great slide of snow — would break free from one of the high peaks. It would come crashing down the mountain and bury anyone who was in its path.

The dogs were especially important at times like this. A dog could smell people even when they were buried under the snow. Then he would bark loudly, and the monks would come running.

All winter Barry and the other dogs learned their lessons. And before long the monks began to watch Barry very carefully. There was something special about the dog. He learned much faster than the others. But that was not enough. Would Barry also be brave? Could the monks trust him as a rescue dog?

At last the lessons were over, and Barry went to work. One afternoon he was trotting ahead of a long line of workmen, leading them through the pass. There was a loud booming noise. It was the beginning of an avalanche!

Barry had never heard this sound before. But somehow he knew that something terrible was about to happen. He raced ahead, barking. Then he circled back around the men. He was trying to get them to move faster. And the men tried. But the last three didn't make it. Moments later the avalanche rolled down over the trail — and the three men were buried under it.

They were probably still alive. It is possible to breathe under snow, but not for long.

Barry looked at the snowy spot for a moment. Then he bounded away. A few minutes later he dashed into the courtyard of the monastery. The monks came running when they heard his frantic barks. *"It's trouble I can't handle alone!"* those barks meant. *"Follow me!"* Then he started out into the snow again.

The monks followed Barry back to where the avalanche had slid across the path. And the men who had gotten through safely told them what had happened.

"Find them, Barry," a monk ordered.

Barry began to sniff across the snow. Suddenly he barked. One of the monks ran over. Carefully he poked a long pole down into the snow. Nothing. He moved a few feet and poked again. Still nothing. So he tried a third time — and gave a shout. "Here!"

Other monks began to dig. A few minutes later the man was free. He was shivering and blue with cold, but he was alive! Soon the other two men were saved too.

That night everyone — the monks and the rescued men — made a big fuss over Barry. They praised him. They petted him. They gave him a large bowl of juicy meat scraps. And the monks nodded to one another. They had been right. This was going to be a *very* special dog.

One day Barry was out on patrol. He saw a small mound of snow. Something was sticking out of that mound — something that looked like the end of a red scarf. Barry raced over. He saw now that the mound was a little girl! She lay curled up in the snow. Barry poked her. Was she still alive? She was. But the cold had made her very weak and sleepy.

Once more Barry seemed to know just what to do. He didn't run back to the monastery this time. He lay down beside the little girl instead. He half covered her with his warm, furry body. And he began to lick her face with his big, rough tongue.

At first the girl didn't move. But slowly as she grew warmer she began to stir. She snuggled under Barry's belly. And she opened her eyes.

She wasn't frightened. She knew right away the big dog was a friend. She continued to snuggle close to his side — and slowly his warmth woke her up. But she was still too weak to stand.

Barry looked around. It was very cold now. But when the sun went down it would be much, much colder.

Barry tugged at the girl's coat. He stood up. He lay down beside her again. It was as if he were telling her something. And maybe he was. Because now the little girl threw one leg around Barry's body. She wrapped her arms around his furry neck. And a few minutes later the St. Bernard padded slowly into the courtyard of the monastery with the little girl riding on his back!

Stories like this soon made Barry famous on both sides of the mountains. Barry just went on doing his job. He did it for more than twelve years. And during that time he helped save the lives of 42 people.

But the work was hard and the

weather was harsh. Soon after Barry's
twelfth birthday the monks noticed that
the dog was growing stiff and slow.

Most old dogs were sent to homes in
the warmer valleys below. But the
monks couldn't bear to part with Barry.
So he stayed at the monastery for several more years.

Then winter came once more. One wild and stormy night Barry was sleeping by the fire. There was a lull in the storm. The monks heard nothing. But Barry's ears were still sharp. Suddenly he was wide awake. He moved to the door and began to whine.

The monks thought he wanted to go into the courtyard. But when they opened the door Barry dashed away into the night.

Not far away Barry found what he was looking for — a man lying face downward in the snow. The man must have shouted a few minutes before. But now he lay very still with his eyes closed.

Barry bent over him. The man rolled over. He half opened his eyes. And what he saw made him scream. A big, dim shape was looming over him! "It's a wolf!" the man thought. With the last of his strength he pulled out his knife — and stuck it deep into Barry's side. Then he fainted again.

The old dog was badly wounded. But

he still had a job to do. Somehow Barry got back to the monastery. He sank to the ground. And the monks, lanterns held high, followed his paw prints — and drops of blood — back to the man.

They were in time to save the man's life. But no one was happy at the monastery that night. The monks took turns looking after Barry. At first they thought he would surely die. But finally he grew a little stronger.

Barry grew stronger, but he was never really well again. And he died a few months later.

The monks and the big St. Bernards still live in the high mountains of Switzerland. But life at the monastery is very different now. Far below, a tunnel goes through the mountain. And a safe road has been built through the pass nearby.

So the dogs are no longer needed for rescue work. But Barry has not been forgotten. Every few years an especially lively and intelligent pup is born at the monastery. He is always named Barry.

Balto,
the dog who saved Nome

"THIS IS NOME, ALASKA. REPEAT. THIS IS NOME, ALASKA. WE NEED HELP. FAST . . ."

A man bent over the machine in the Nome telegraph office. Again and again he pressed down the signal key. *Click-click-clack . . . Clack-click-clack . . .* He was sending a message to the town of Anchorage, Alaska, 800 miles to the south.

Click-click-clack . . . Clack-click-clack . . . The Anchorage telegraph operator wrote down the message. The news was very bad.

A terrible sickness had broken out in the Nome area — a disease called diphtheria. Some people had already died of it. Many more would die if they weren't treated soon.

There was no medicine to treat diphtheria in Nome. The medicine they needed would have to come from Anchorage — 800 miles away — through a wild wind and snow storm. The storm was so bad that airplanes couldn't fly through it. Trains couldn't get through either. Nome was very near the sea, but the sea was frozen solid. And the road from the south was completely blocked by deep drifts of snow.

There was only one way to get the medicine from Anchorage to Nome — by dogsled.

The medicine was packed in a box and sent north by train — as far as a train could go on the snowy tracks. It was still more than 600 miles south of Nome. From now on teams of dogs would have to take it the rest of the way.

The teams were ready. The first team pushed north through the storm to a little town. There a second team was waiting. It went on to another small town where a third team was ready to take the medicine on north.

At first the teams managed to go many miles before they grew tired. But the storm was growing worse by the minute. Finally Charlie Olson's team staggered into the little village of Bluff — 60 miles south of Nome. They had only gone 20 miles, yet Olson and the dogs were almost frozen and completely worn out.

Gunnar Kasson and his team were waiting in Bluff. The wind screamed through the little town. The snow was piling up deeper and deeper on the ground. It was 30 degrees *below* zero

Fahrenheit outside now. And the temperature was falling fast.

"It's no use trying to go out in *that*," Charlie Olson said. "I almost didn't make it. You and the dogs will freeze solid before you get half way."

But Kasson knew how important the medicine was. He knew that hundreds — maybe thousands — of people would die if they didn't get the medicine soon. Besides, he knew he didn't have to go all the way. Another team was waiting 40 miles north in the little village of Safety. That team would take the medicine the last 20 miles to Nome.

Quickly Gunnar Kasson hitched up his team of dogs. And at the head of the long line he put his lead dog, Balto.

Balto was a mixed-breed. He was half Eskimo dog — and half wolf. Many dogs who are part wolf never become tame. They never learn to trust people — or obey them either. Balto was different. He was a gentle dog who obeyed orders quickly. He also knew how to think for himself.

Usually Gunnar Kasson guided the dogs. He told them where to go. Now he couldn't even see his hand in front of his face. So everything was up to Balto. The big black dog would have to find the trail by smell. Then he'd have to stay on it no matter what happened.

Gunnar Kasson climbed onto the back of the sled. He cracked his whip in the air. *"Mush!"* he cried. *"Move out!"*

The first part of the trail to Nome led across the sea ice. This ice wasn't anything like ice on a small pond or lake. It seemed much more *alive*. And no wonder. The water *under* the ice was moving up and down because of the storm. So the ice was moving up and down too. Up and down, up and down it went, like a roller coaster.

In some places the ice was smooth —
as smooth and slippery as glass. Dogs
are usually sure-footed. But they slipped
and skidded across this ice. So did the
sled.

And sometimes the ice came to sharp
points — points that dug deep into the
dogs' paws.

Worst of all were the places where
the ice was bumpy — so bumpy that the
sled turned over again and again. Each
time it turned over the other dogs began to bark and snap at each other. But
Balto always stood quietly while Kasson set the sled upright again. Balto was
calm, so the other dogs grew calmer too.

The team had been moving across the
ice for hours. Suddenly there was a loud
cracking sound — like a gun going off.
Kasson knew that sound. It was the
sound of ice breaking. Somewhere not
far ahead the ice had split apart. If the

team kept going straight they would run right into the freezing water — and drown.

Balto heard the ice crack too. He slowed for a moment. Then he turned left. He headed straight out to sea. He went for a long time. Then he turned right once more.

Balto was leading the team *around* the icy water. Finally he gave a sharp bark and turned north. He had found the trail to Nome again.

Soon the trail left the sea ice. From now on it was over land. Things should have been easier. They weren't. The snow was falling thick and fast. In some places the wind swept most of it off the trail. But in other places the snow drifts came up almost over the dogs' heads. And the wind was blowing harder and harder. It sent bits of icy snow straight into Kasson's eyes. "I might as well have been blind," he said. "I couldn't even *guess* where we were."

And the dogs were so tired! Again and again they tried to stop. They wanted to lie down and go to sleep in the snow. Balto was just as tired. But he would not stop. He kept on pulling — and the other dogs had to follow behind.

Now something else began to worry Gunnar Kasson. They had been traveling for about 14 hours. Surely they should have reached the town of Safety in 14 hours. Kasson went on for another hour. Then he knew. Somehow they had missed the town in the storm. They must have passed right by the new dog team!

Kasson knew they couldn't stop and wait for the storm to die down. He and the dogs would freeze if they did. They couldn't go back to Bluff either. They had come too far. There was only one thing to do now. Pray . . . and push on to Nome.

Later Gunnar Kasson said he couldn't remember those last miles very well. Each one was a nightmare of howling wind and swirling snow and bitter cold. But somehow — with Balto leading slowly and steadily — they made it! At 5:30 in the morning, February 2, 1925 —

after 20 hours on the trail — the team limped into Nome!

The whole town was waiting for the medicine! They gathered around Gunnar Kasson. They shook his hand and pounded him on the back. "How can we ever thank you?" one woman cried.

Gunnar Kasson shook his head. Then he sank to his knees beside Balto. He began to pull long splinters of ice from the dog's paws. "Balto, what a dog," he

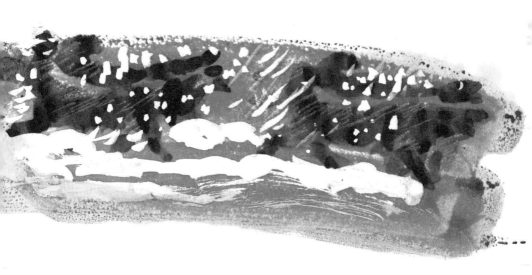

said. "I've been in Alaska for 20 years and this was the toughest trip I've ever made. But Balto, *he* brought us through."

Many newspaper and magazine stories were written about Balto. His picture was printed on postcards and in books. And today, on a grassy hill in New York City's Central Park, there is a life-sized statue of Balto — the dog who saved Nome.

Silver and Sascha,
a blind dog and her friend

Silver had always been a happy dog. She loved people petting her. She loved chasing balls and sticks. She was always eager to play games like "You run after me — then I'll run after you" with other dogs. But something was happening to Silver.

The collie lived with many other dogs in a kennel near the city of Chicago. All sorts of dogs were born and raised there to be sold as pets. But Michael von Motzeck, the man who ran the kennel, never thought of selling Silver. She was such a good-looking dog. She was small and slim and her three-color coat was thick and shiny. Mr. von Motzeck wanted her to stay at the kennel and give him many litters of good-looking collie pups.

But Silver was acting oddly. She never raced around the big kennel yard any more. She was walking very strangely too — stiff-legged and slow. She didn't play with the other dogs. Sometimes she even growled if one suddenly came too close. When somebody threw a ball she didn't try to catch it. And she spent more and more time lying alone in some corner.

Mr. von Motzeck grew more and more worried. What could all this mean? Finally he took Silver to a veterinarian. The doctor examined her. His news was bad. Silver was fast going blind. "And there's nothing I can do," the veterinarian added.

Mr. von Motzeck took Silver home. He was more worried than ever now. He knew that being blind didn't bother some dogs. They could still get around by using their keen senses of hearing and smell. But he also knew that other dogs became terribly unhappy. So unhappy that they often stopped eating and died.

Mr. von Motzeck didn't want this to happen to Silver. He was very fond of her. And she was only five years old. But what could he do to make her life happier? Suddenly Mr. von Motzeck had an idea. Some blind people had guide dogs to help them get around — dogs that served as their eyes. And *he* had a kennel full of dogs. What if he found a guide dog for Silver too?

But which dog? Mr. von Motzeck knew that a guide dog had to have certain traits. Guide dogs had to be friendly. They had to be calm. They had to be smart. Most of all they had to be *dependable.* They couldn't run off to play with another dog or chase a cat when they were working.

Mr. von Motzeck wandered around the kennel. He looked at dog after dog. And again and again he shook his head. One was too shy. Another wasn't smart enough. A third was too lazy. Finally Mr. von Motzeck stopped in front of a three-year-old dachshund named Sascha. "Yes," he thought. "Sascha's the one. She has all the traits a guide dog should have. Best of all she has a good heart."

Then Mr. von Motzeck had to train Sascha. But how? No one had ever trained a guide dog for a dog before. What if Sascha didn't understand what she was supposed to do? What if Silver refused to go along with Sascha? Mr. von Motzeck gave himself a little shake. It was time to stop asking such questions. There was only one thing he could do now. Try — and hope for the best.

First Mr. von Motzeck found a rope and tied one end to Sascha's collar. He tied the other end to Silver's. "Come Sascha," he called. Then he led the dachshund down the street — with Silver training behind.

At first Silver balked. She pulled back on the rope. She tried to sit down. She turned and tried to go back to the kennel. But Mr. von Motzeck wouldn't let her. And after a while Silver stopped balking. Somehow she seemed to sense that she wasn't bumping into so many things with Sascha moving ahead of her.

Now Mr. von Motzeck began to teach Sascha the things every guide dog must know. He taught her to stop at every street corner and look right and left for cars. He taught her to wait until there was no traffic in the street. *Then* she could lead Silver across.

He taught her to lead Silver safely around things that were in the way — garbage cans and mailboxes and lamp posts and people. Most of all he taught Sascha that Silver was her job. When she was by herself she could do any doggy thing she wanted to. But when she was tied to Silver she must understand that she was a *working* dog.

And how did Sascha like all this training? She loved it! And she grew closer and closer to Silver too. Before long the two dogs were taking long walks by themselves. They trotted along the street,

sniffed at store windows and even ran and played in the park. Soon more and more people began to call out as they passed, "Hello, Sascha! Hello, Silver!"

Mr. von Motzeck always untied the rope between Sascha and Silver when the dogs were at home. But still they worked as a team. Sascha usually stayed close by so Silver could smell the dachshund's special dog smell. And often Silver could also hear the sound of Sascha's toe-nails as they *click-clicked* across the floor.

Every evening Silver and Sascha ate dinner from the same big bowl. Then they curled up close together on a blanket they shared as a bed.

Gone were the days when Silver stumbled or bumped into things. Gone were the days when she spent so many sad hours alone. Silver was a happy dog once more — because of her spare pair of eyes.

Bobbie,
the dog who would not give up

Bobbie was born on a farm in the western state of Oregon. The roly-poly little collie grew up chasing chickens and sniffing wonderful smells in the barnyard and wandering for hours through the nearby fields and woods.

Then the Braziers — the people Bobbie lived with — moved to a nearby town. The chickens and the barn, the fields and the woods, were gone. But Bobbie didn't seem to mind. He was the kind of dog who could be happy almost anywhere —

as long as he was near his human family.

In the summer of 1923 the Braziers decided to take a long car trip. Slowly they drove east across the United States — Mr. and Mrs. Brazier, their two children, and Bobbie.

One hot August day they came to the mid-west town of Wolcott, Indiana. Mr. Brazier saw that the gas tank was almost empty. "Might as well stop for some gas," he said, "and Bobbie can have a run, too."

Mr. Brazier pulled into a gas station. Mrs. Brazier opened the door and Bobbie jumped out. "Don't go far," one of the children called as he trotted away. But no one was really worried. Bobbie had run free all his life — and never gone too far.

But just then a big, mean looking dog came by. When he saw Bobbie he crouched — and began to growl. *"Let's fight!"* that growl seemed to say. And Bobbie growled back. Now the dog began to back away. Suddenly he turned and ran down the street — and Bobbie ran after him.

When it was time to leave, Mr. Brazier gave a sharp whistle — expecting to see the big collie dash toward them. But he didn't. The children called "Bobbie! Bobbie!" again and again. And still the dog did not come into sight.

"Where could he be?" said Mrs. Brazier. The family waited for a long time. Finally, they decided to look for Bobbie. First they walked up and down nearby streets calling his name. Then they went from house to house all over the neighborhood. But no one had seen Bobbie. "Maybe someone has stolen him," one man said. "Or maybe he's been hit by a car." When the children heard this they burst into tears.

Then Mr. Brazier took his family to the town's newspaper office. He told a reporter there the story. And he offered a reward. "We'll pay it to anyone who finds him and lets us know," he said. Now there was nothing else to do. A few minutes later four very unhappy people got into their car and drove out of town.

The Braziers continued their vacation and then returned to Oregon. It seemed strange and sad to be back home without their pet. Time passed. It was the fall of 1923. Then it was winter. Then it was February 15, 1924 — exactly six months to the day since Bobbie had been left behind in Wolcott, Indiana.

The time was late afternoon. A dog came limping up the street. He was so thin his bones showed through his matted fur. His eyes were dull and his body was covered with raw patches. The dog turned in at the Braziers'. Slowly he climbed the porch steps. He stood there for a few moments. Then his legs folded under him and he sank to the floor.

A few minutes later one of the Brazier children came out of the house. She stared

at the dog. The dog's tail moved a little. It made a soft, thumping sound against the wooden porch. Suddenly the girl's eyes grew wide. "Bobbie!" she cried. "It's Bobbie!"

And it was! Somehow Bobbie had found his way home! But it had taken all his strength to do it. Again and again he tried to stand. But his legs were too weak. All he could do was wag his tail a little — and lick the hands that were petting him.

Quickly the Braziers made a soft bed of blankets for him next to the kitchen stove. For the next few days they fed Bobbie small meals of warm milk and eggs and soft pieces of bread. And very slowly the collie grew stronger.

The Braziers told many of their friends about Bobbie. And before long other people began to hear about his amazing journey too. A newspaper reporter in the nearby city of Portland wrote a story about it. Then other magazines and newspapers wrote stories too. Suddenly Bobbie was famous!

More and more people began to make special trips to see the dog. Before they left they usually asked the Braziers two questions. First, *where* had Bobbie been? What kind of country had he passed through on his long trip home? And second, *how* had he done it? How had he managed to cross three thousand miles of land he'd never seen before — and find his way back to one small town?

The Braziers were able to answer the first question — or at least parts of it. A number of people who had read about Bobbie wrote letters to them. They told of seeing the collie at different times on his trip west. A woman living near St. Louis, Missouri wrote that Bobbie had stopped at her house in the late summer of 1923. He'd stayed for a few days — then one morning he was gone.

Another letter came from a small town

near Des Moines. Once more Bobbie had stopped for a while. Once more he'd been fed and petted. And once more he'd disappeared very soon.

Another letter came from much farther west. A man had been on a fishing trip in the Rocky Mountains of Colorado. One evening a very thin collie had limped into his camp. The man fed the dog — and before long he grew very fond of him too. "I'll take him home with me when it's time to go," the man decided. But on the last morning of his trip he woke — to find Bobbie gone.

The Braziers used these — and other letters — to make a map of Bobbie's trip west. It was a rough map. Often Bobbie had gone many hundreds of miles — and nobody wrote to say he'd been seen. But the Braziers knew that Bobbie had passed through many cities and towns. He had crossed farms and forests. He had waded in streams and swum deep rivers. He had climbed over the Rocky Mountains in the late fall of the year. How deep the snow must have been on those high peaks then! He had plodded through mile after sandy mile of the Great Salt Lake Desert.

The Braziers could also imagine many of the things that had happened to Bobbie along the way. Some people had been very good to him, true. But many others wouldn't want to bother with a strange dog — especially such a thin and dirty looking one.

So Bobbie must have spent most of his time alone. Very likely he went for days without food or water. And probably most of what he did eat came from garbage cans. Yet nothing had stopped him—not mountains or deserts or hunger or pain or bone-tiredness. Against all odds, he had made his way home again!

But *how?* How had he managed to cross those thousands of miles of land he'd never seen before?

This was not such an easy question to answer! Some scientists said they thought Bobbie could tell where he was by the sun and the stars. Others said animals like Bobbie might have an *extra* built-in sense — like the sense of hearing or smell — to help guide them where they wanted to go. A few people even said that perhaps Bobbie could "home in" on the Brazier family's *minds*. Somehow he could tell where his loved ones were.

But no one really knew the answer to the question of how Bobbie made his incredible journey then — and no one knows today. All we know is he did. Somehow Bobbie *cared* enough to find his family again.

Bibliography

BOOKS

Baker, Peter Shaw. *Dog Heroes*. London, England: Ward, Lock and Company Ltd., 1935.

Downey, Fairfax, selected by. *Dogs of Destiny*. Garden City, New York: Doubleday and Company, Inc., 1962.

Fiennes, Richard and Alice. *The Natural History of Dogs*. New York: Doubleday & Company, Inc., 1968.

Fox, Dr. Michael. *Understanding Your Dog*. New York: Coward, McCann & Geoghegan, Inc., 1972.

Handel, Leo. *A Dog Named Duke, True Stories of German Shepherds At Work with the Law*. Philadelphia, Pennsylvania: J.B. Lippincott Company, 1966.

Hurlimann, Bettina, and Nessbaumer, Paul. *Barry, The Story of a Brave St. Bernard.* New York: Harcourt, Brace & World, 1967.

Johns, Rowland. *Dogs You'd Like To Meet.* London, England: Methuen and Company Ltd., 1924.

Lorenz, Konrad. *Man Meets Dog.* Harmondsworth, Middlesex, England: Penguin Books, 1964.

Mahir, Tom. *Police Dogs At Work.* London, England: J.M. Dent and Sons Ltd., 1970.

Pease, Eleanor Fairchild. *Heroes All, More Tales of Real Dogs.* Chicago, Illinois: Albert Whitman and Company, 1940.

Terhune, Albert Payson. *Real Tales of Real Dogs.* Akron, Ohio: The Sealfield Publishing Company, 1935.

Thorne, Diane, and Terhune, Albert Payson. *The Dog Book.* Akron, Ohio: The Sealfield Publishing Company, 1937.

MAGAZINES

"Canny Canines, Items from the American Kennel Gazette." *Reader's Digest,* March, 1943, pp. 78–9.

"Caution: Dogs at Work." *Colliers Magazine,* February 20, 1927, pp. 11+.

"Dog Leads Blind Dog." *Life Magazine,* April 9, 1945, pp. 130–2.

"Dogs of Duty and Devotion." *National Geographic Magazine,* December, 1941, pp. 769–806.

"Dogs of Fame and Some Not So Famous." *Nature Magazine*, February, 1940, pp. 87+.

"Four Footed Cops." *Saturday Evening Post*, September 22, 1956, pp. 38–9+.

"Greatest Detective in Dogdom; Dox of Italy." *Reader's Digest*, August, 1960, pp. 57–60.

"Profiles: American Kennel Club." *New Yorker Magazine*, December, 1941, pp. 31–4.

"Racing the Black Death of Alaska." *Literary Digest*, February 21, 1925, pp. 42–8.

"Saints of the Frozen Alps." *House & Garden Magazine*, November, 1933, pp. 9–11.

"Seeing Eye Dog for a Dog." *Science Digest*, March, 1969, p. 39.

"Switzerland's Avalanche Dogs." *Reader's Digest*, December, 1956, pp. 145–9.

"Wolf's Day Off." *Goodhousekeeping Magazine*, March, 1924, p. 9.

"Wolf, Son of Lad, Saves His Friends." *Goodhousekeeping Magazine*, April, 1924, pp. 52–3.

"Working Like a Dog: Strange Lives Some Dogs Lead." *Better Homes and Gardens*, May, 1941, pp. 99+.

Index